F.

A Book about a Boy with AUTISM

Mori's Story

Zachary M. Gartenberg
Photographs by Jerry Gay

⌐ LERNER PUBLICATIONS COMPANY / MINNEAPOLIS

This book is dedicated to my dear brother, Moriel Nachum Gartenberg.

I would like to acknowledge my mother, Celia Gartenberg, who worked with me to edit and revise the manuscript at each stage, and who typed all its drafts. My grandmother Lael Cohen took several of the photographs in the book. My grandmother Ina Gartenberg and my cousin Debbie Kleid are my heroes for acting as my agents. Without their efforts, this book would not have been published. Thanks to the people who shared their feelings with me.

Text copyright © 1998 by Lerner Publications Company
Photographs copyright © 1998 by Jerry Gay
Photographs on pp. 11, 12, 23, 24, 26 courtesy of Lael Cohen

Website address: www.lernerbooks.com

LIBRARY OF CONGRESS CATALOGING-IN-PUBLICATION DATA

Gartenberg, Zachary M.
     Mori's story : A book about a boy with autism / Zachary M. Gartenberg ; photographs by Jerry Gay.
        p. cm.
     Summary: a boy discusses his autistic brother, including his home life, foster home, schooling, and how the disease affects the whole family.
     ISBN 0-8225-2585-2 (alk. paper)
     1. Autism in children—Juvenile literature. [1. Autism.
2. Diseases. 3. Children's writings.] I. Gay, Jerry, ill.
II. Title.
RJ506.A9G37   1998
362.2'6—dc21   97-33495

Manufactured in the United States of America
1 2 3 4 5 6 – JR – 03 02 01 00 99 98

CONTENTS

THIS IS A STORY ABOUT MY BROTHER, Moriel. Moriel has autism. My parents gave him a Hebrew name which means "God is my teacher." I think they just thought the name was beautiful, but its meaning came true in a way they didn't expect. Moriel teaches others that people with disabilities, such as autism, can accomplish many things. I think God wants us to understand that there are different kinds of people, and nobody's perfect. Anyway, we call my brother Mori for short.

My name is Zach. My family and I live in Seattle, Washington. My father is a rabbi. A rabbi is someone who teaches people about the Jewish religion. He's like a priest or a minister, only for a Jewish congregation. My mother sometimes works as a cantor. A cantor sings the religious music in a synagogue. Like a church, a synagogue is where Jewish people gather to pray.

Mori is nine years old. I'm almost eleven, and my sister, Fay, is seven. For the last couple years, Mori has not lived at home with the rest of us. He lives in a group home for children who have different kinds of disabilities. A group home is a place where people with special needs can get care that is just right for them. Mori stays with us two weekends a month, on holidays, and for two weeks in the summer. We really look forward to his visits.

Some people think that if there is something wrong with a person's brain or if they behave strangely, they should have to stay in a hospital or in an institution where they won't bother anybody. But many people with disabilities live in a home like the one my brother lives in.

The people who take care of Mori are a husband and wife, Nancy and Ed Peterson. They get paid by the government to take care of children and adults with disabilities. Nancy and Ed have been doing this work for 20 years, even while they were raising their own children. They've worked with several other kids with autism—kids like Mori.

People who have autism are all unique, but one thing they have in common is that they see the world differently than most of us do. That makes them act strangely sometimes. They also can't learn to talk very easily. The reason they are different from most of us has something to do with their brains. With autism, a person's brain doesn't work the way a brain usually does.

My brother could talk until he was about two years old. After that he couldn't talk at all. He still can't. That happens to lots of autistic kids. Some of them learn to talk, but they talk in a strange way, like they'll repeat what you say, or they'll say "you" when they mean "I."

Although Mori doesn't use words to communicate, he sings a lot and makes funny noises. He also uses his body to tell us what he wants. When he was little, he would take us by the hand, lead us to the refrigerator, and point to what he wanted to eat. Now that he's older, he can use some sign language if he wants to eat or drink, or he can show a picture of what he wants.

Mori has to take special medicine so he can stay calm. When he doesn't have his medicine, he has screaming fits and might bang his head on the floor. He also goes around wrecking things in the house—throwing food, spilling toys, pulling down curtains. He especially likes to take apart mattresses and stuffed toys. You can imagine that this behavior is hard to live with, and it can get expensive.

Mori will also keep doing the same thing over and over, even if you tell him to stop. He can't be left alone because he might do something annoying or dangerous. Once he grabbed a lady's ice cream right off her cone. He climbed out the car window to do it, and it only took a second! He's really fast and unpredictable.

Some people think that if you're autistic, you just sit in a room and spin plates or something. But Mori loves to be with people. He looks at us and laughs and gives hugs and kisses. Mori used to wander around the room and ignore what other people were doing, but now when my dad wrestles with us, Mori jumps right in. He also plays ball, rides a tricycle, and in-line skates. He's also really good at riding horses—better than me, because he takes lessons. He can't swim yet, but he loves being in the pool.

WHEN MORI WAS BORN, my mother asked the nurse if he was retarded. My mom says she just had a funny feeling when she looked at Mori—he was very quiet and his eyes seemed to be shaped differently. She thought he might have Down syndrome, a form of mental retardation. But the nurse said, "Of course not!" So my mother didn't worry about it anymore.

My mother was working as a cantor when Mori was born. When he was one month old, she took him with her to choir rehearsals for some important religious services. She put him down on stage while she directed the choir. When the choir sang a high note, Mori would squeak out loud in the right tune.

As a baby, Mori loved to be swung up and down by his feet. When he was a toddler, my mother played a game called "I love you." She would get far away from us and hold her arms open. Mori and I ran as fast as we could while she said the word "I." When we got to her she would catch us in her arms and say "love you!" Mori loved this game and would run to her from very far away.

When Mori was almost a year old, we went to Israel to visit our cousins who live in Jerusalem. Mori had his first birthday party there. He got a colorful stuffed caterpillar, and our aunt made chocolate cupcakes. We learned how to speak a little Hebrew. Hebrew is the main language in Israel.

When Mori was a year and a half old, his favorite word was havdalah. That's a little ceremony we have at the end of our Sabbath every week. We light a candle and sing some songs. Mori would point to the havdalah candle and get very excited. He could count to ten in Hebrew and English. Mori and I went to the Jewish Community Center preschool, where my mother taught. Mori liked to play with his friends and run around outdoors. It was a very happy time in our lives.

But sometime before Mori was two years old, things changed. He stopped talking and started acting really weird. After a short time, he didn't use words at all. He would only cry, sing, and point to get what he wanted. When he ate, he spit out all his food, dropped his plate on the floor, and smeared his food all over his clothes.

He cried and threw tantrums all the time. Sometimes if my mom rocked him in the rocking chair, he jumped out of her lap. He had very odd finger movements. He would put his pointer finger next to his eye and his thumb next to his ear. When he did that, he would sing a funny tune: "Yu-bu-bu-bu-bu-bu-do-do-do-do." He wouldn't look at anyone or play games like patty-cake or peekaboo. He didn't pay attention to things the way the other little kids did. He just stared off into space, kind of out of it. My mom and dad said it seemed like Mori had an electrical wire in his brain that was plugged in at times, and unplugged other times.

My parents took him to the doctor. The doctor gave him lots of tests. They tested him for genetic problems. Genetic problems have to do with the way you are made in your cells even before you are born. You can inherit things like blue eyes or blond hair because of the genes in your family. Some doctors think that autism works that way, too. My parents were very nervous while they waited for the results of the tests.

The doctor sent Mori to a special school while my parents were waiting to find out what was wrong. The school was for children who were not developing normally.

One day, my parents were watching Mori in the classroom. Another parent was watching her child, too. She talked about her child and it sounded like she was talking about Mori. My parents asked her what problem her child had. She said it was autism. So my mom and dad took Mori to another doctor, and the doctor said he did have autism. My parents felt a little relieved that they finally knew what was wrong with Mori. But they were also very, very sad. My father cried.

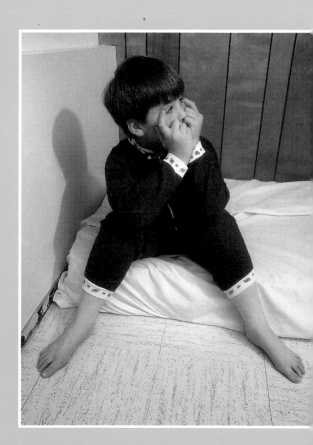

I remember that my parents talked about Mori all the time. I asked them questions, too. I wondered if Mori would ever be able to talk. My parents told me that he talks in his own way. They hope that someday he will talk in a normal way. My sister asks if Mori will ever get married. My mom sort of doubts it. People with autism have a hard time relating to people.

Once my parents knew more about what was going on, they started getting help. They got advice from lots of people. Sometimes they got confused about what to do. Everything they needed to do cost a lot of money. They got help from the state government. The government helps pay for things that people with disabilities need.

My parents bought special equipment so that Heidi, who is a physical therapist, could work with Mori at our house. They installed a hammock, a soft bouncy swing, and a platform swing. The house looked kind of weird, but we had tons of fun on the equipment. Mori, Fay, and I would fall asleep in the hammock together. Once my friend Justin came over and he, Mori, and I swung in the hammock in front of the fireplace while my dad made hamburgers for us.

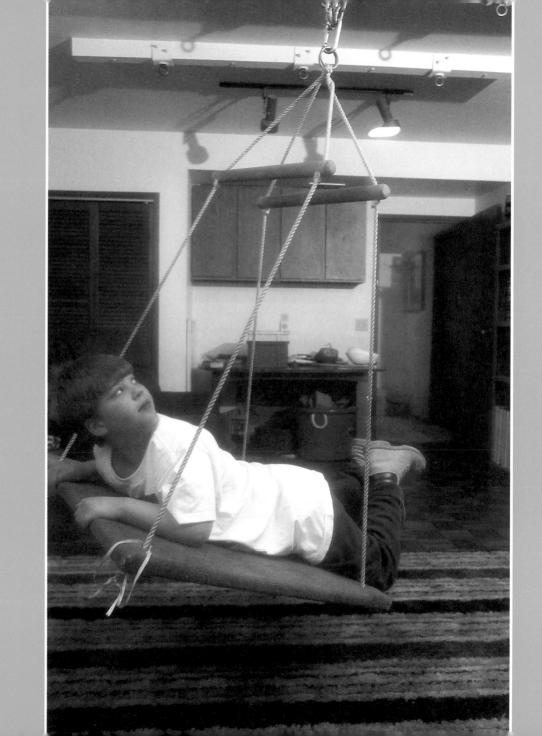

My parents tried lots of things to help Mori get better, like giving him certain vitamins and taking him to get his head rubbed a special way. The head rubbing is called "cranial-sacral therapy." They also took him to get training in how to listen better. He had to wear earphones twice a day for ten days and listen to special sounds. The training works for some people with autism, but it didn't seem to help Mori.

SOMETIMES MORI ACTED in ways that were very difficult for my family to handle. He pulled down the window drapes. He pulled up flowers from my mom's garden. He ate rotten apples that fell from our tree. He kept running into the neighbors' yard to eat their strawberries, so we had to put up a fence. We also had to put locks on all the doors in the house so he wouldn't get into things.

Mori would smear crayons and marking pens all over the walls and stuff them into his mouth. His tongue would be all different colors. When Mori ate, we had to pin his left sleeve to his pant leg so he wouldn't mess up his food. He would grab ice cream out of the refrigerator, dump it, and eat it off the floor.

Once we could not find Mori. We searched for about an hour, and finally we found him three blocks away. He was running down the middle of a busy street. Another time he climbed out a second-story window and onto the roof. Even though he climbed all the time, he never fell.

Mori would grab food and soda cans from strangers. Some people thought it was funny. But one time, in a bakery, Mori smeared his cupcake frosting on a man's pants. The man got mad and made my mom give him money for cleaning the pants. When things like that happened, my mom would get in a pretty bad mood. We would have to leave her alone. That made me feel lonely and worried.

Mori could not use the toilet until just this year. At night, he still wears diapers. We have to put him in special pajamas that are pinned up so he can't take them off.

For my parents, the hardest times were when Mori would scream, throw himself on the ground, and bang his head. Once my mother tried to give him some pills that were supposed to calm him down. He screamed and squirmed so hard that my mother felt like hitting him! She hit the floor instead. She really wanted to help him, but she couldn't.

Mori still does these things, but instead of doing them almost all the time like he did when he was younger, he only does them once in a while. We think his behavior has improved because he's living in a good environment, he has the right medication, and he's getting lots of his needs met.

WHEN MORI WAS FOUR YEARS OLD, he went to live at a special home for children with behavior problems. Two women ran the program. They changed Mori's diet, and they were very firm with him. They didn't let him do whatever he wanted.

After Mori had been there for about a month, he started changing. He was calmer and better behaved. He slept in his own bed instead of on the floor. He ate neatly for the first time. We saw Mori sitting quietly in a chair, which he never used to do at home. My parents said it was like a gift that he was getting better.

My parents also took a class to learn how to deal with Mori. They learned not to overreact when Mori misbehaved. They were taught just to ignore his behavior. This was very hard. After that, when my parents got mad at Mori, they yelled at each other instead of him. But the teachers told them that part of the reason Mori acted up was to get us to yell and make a big fuss. So my mom and dad tried to be more calm around him.

Mori was at this place for about four months—then he came home. But my mom and dad still needed help, so Mori stayed with another family on weekends and after school. Their names are Sue and Yijun. They are from China. Every time I went over there, we all watched movies and ate homemade Chinese food. Sue and Yijun took care of Mori for four years.

When my brother was seven years old, our family was planning to go to Israel for a year for my dad's work. My parents wanted me and my sister to spend a school year in Israel, but it was hard to decide what to do with Mori. They weren't sure he could go on the plane with us and make such a big change in his life. One thing that really upsets Mori is a change in his routine. Life in Israel would be very different than here. Mori has difficulty relating to people and adjusting to new things. Even though he would be with his family in Israel, the change in cultures would be too different.

After a lot of thinking, my parents finally decided that it would be impossible to get him settled in a strange place. But where would he live if he stayed in Seattle? That's when we found out about Nancy and Ed Peterson. Mori lived with them for a while before we left. It looked like it would work out. But Mori still had a hard time adjusting to his new home.

Right before we left for Israel, Mori, Fay, and I went to an amusement park together. There were a lot of rides. I personally didn't enjoy rides. I'd rather have a nice quiet time on my own with Mori. On the way home I couldn't stop crying. I cried for two reasons—because I was going away and wouldn't see my brother for a long time, and because I didn't have a very good time at the amusement park. It was supposed to be a good-bye present.

A YEAR LATER, WHEN WE RETURNED FROM ISRAEL, Mori was doing well at Nancy and Ed's house. He seemed happy, so we decided to keep him there. Mori has a busy schedule at their house, but it is always the same routine, with lots of structure. And someone is always there to pay attention to him. My parents say they can't do that and still take care of me and my sister. Not all parents of kids with autism have them live with another family. Sometimes the kids stay at home. But this decision was right for our family, even though it was hard.

Nancy and Ed give kids like Mori everything they need, but they also expect them to behave well. A couple other kids also live with Nancy and Ed. Jessica is Mori's age, and she's very cute. She can speak and doesn't have the same problems as Mori, but she is still disabled. Aaron can't move, talk, or hear. Nancy and Ed's cat, Dusqueak, sits on Aaron's stomach when he is lying in bed. Aaron and Jessica love to have Mori around because he is funny and entertaining.

Nancy and Ed have a nice backyard and a tree house. Mori has his own room with glow-in-the-dark stars and a little doll hanging from the ceiling. Sometimes he wakes up in the middle of the night. He usually just makes noises but doesn't leave his room.

Nancy and Ed buy clothes, books, and toys for Mori and Jessica. They also send them to school every day. Mori and Jessica both go to a public school, but they are in different classes. There are only a few kids in Mori's class. They all need extra attention. Mori does some things with kids from regular classes. He has an art buddy. He also has lunch and gym with other kids in the school. The teachers are working on Mori's speech. They are the ones who taught him to use the toilet during the day. This was a big accomplishment for Mori and a big relief for my parents!

The most important thing is that Mori is beginning to talk. He can say "ple" for "please" when he wants something. He is also learning the normal way to behave. His teachers are so helpful. They make learning fun by giving him play time and different types of treats. Some of the treats aren't what you might expect. They let him play with a necklace, squirt water into his mouth with a spray bottle, give him a ball to squeeze, or rub his arm. Mori loves those things and he'll do his schoolwork to get them.

Some people think that people with disabilities are not smart, but my brother is smart. He remembers everything you teach him. He's always eager to learn and then go out and play. I really love him.

Moriel can draw and sing. He is very strong and runs fast. He's pretty good at in-line skating if you hold his hand. He goes to park programs and does all kinds of outdoor activities and artwork. Every summer he goes to an overnight camp called Easter Seals Camp. The kids there all have disabilities. They do neat stuff like archery, boating, and horseback riding.

Mori is learning to ride horses in a program called Little Bit Special Riders. He can do many tricks, like standing up on the horse's back and turning around while the horse is walking. My grandparents pay for the riding lessons. Nancy has to drive a long way to take him there, but she says it's worth it.

31

This past year, Mori has been learning how to get what he wants by showing cards with pictures and words on them. He can make sentences with them. Once Nancy had a bowl of M&M's candies. Mori ran downstairs and got his "I want" card and gave it to her so he could get some. Another time he threw all his picture cards at Nancy when she wouldn't give him some M&M's. Mori really likes M&M's.

Mori likes to have Sabbath dinner with us. He loves the Challah bread, the chicken, and the grape juice. He knows about Christmas, too, because Nancy and Ed aren't Jewish. But they respect our religion. They make sure Mori gets to light Hanukah candles even when he is at their house. Nancy even bought Mori a blanket with Jewish symbols on it like the Star of David.

Nancy and Ed love Mori as much as my parents do. My mom says it takes two families to raise a kid like Mori! She doesn't know what she'd do if we didn't have Nancy and Ed to help us.

MORI CAN COMMUNICATE MORE EASILY with me than he used to. He hugs me when I hug him. Sometimes he jumps up and down with a happy expression on his face.

When Mori gets upset, it makes me upset. It bothers me that I don't know what he wants or what he's feeling. He doesn't cry about things that hurt him. Once he banged his head against the piano and had to go to the doctor for stitches, and he didn't cry once! What does upset him is when things are different from what he expects.

I sometimes take my video camera to Nancy and Ed's house, or I take notes and study Mori. I don't get to do this very often because I have lots of friends and lots of homework. When I grow up I want to be a movie director, and make a movie about Mori.

34

Information about AUTISM

Autism is a lifelong disability. It usually appears in the first three years of life. It is a disorder that affects how the brain works. Autism and its symptoms occur in about 15 out of every 10,000 births and is four times more common in boys than in girls. It has been found throughout the world in families of all racial, ethnic, and social backgrounds. Autism is not the same as emotional or mental illness, or mental retardation. It can occur along with these things, or with other disorders of the brain, such as seizure disorders.

A person who has autism may show some or all of the following characteristics, or symptoms.

Physical, social, and language skills develop at different ages than they do in people without autism. For example, most three-year-olds play with other children, can use small scissors, and can talk in short sentences. But most three-year-olds with autism aren't able to do these things on their own.

Responses to sensations may be different. People with autism get different impressions from their five senses (sight, hearing, touch, smell, and taste) than people without autism. Their reactions to pain are also different. Things that would hurt a person without autism might not hurt someone with autism. The way a person with autism stands or sits may not seem normal.

People with autism may never talk, or they may use language differently than persons without autism. Even if their speech is abnormal, persons with autism can often do math or art, or remember things better than other people.

Most people learn certain ways of reacting to people, objects, and events. But people with autism don't naturally learn these things and may react differently. For example, they don't understand why it's important to wait before crossing the street. They get used to a certain routine and may get very upset if it is changed. A child with autism often does not play with toys in the usual way, but might take a piece of string and twirl it over and over again.

People with severe cases of autism can act in ways that are harmful to themselves or to things they come into contact with. They may constantly repeat the same actions. People with severe autism need constant supervision and special, safe environments. It is important to remember that they cannot help what they are doing.

Many scientists and educators are doing studies to learn more about autism. Most experts believe that the best way to help people with autism is by using teaching methods that focus on behavior. The teacher helps the student with autism learn normal behavior by rewarding him or her for specific behaviors. The student practices the behavior over and over. The best results happen when these programs are started while the child is still very young.

GLOSSARY

autistic (aw-TISS-tik)—having autism

autism (AW-tizm)—a disorder of the brain that makes it difficult to talk and to relate to other people

disabilities—limitations that interfere with a person's ability to function—for example, to walk, talk, hear, or learn

genetic (juh-NET-ick)—having to do with the information in the body that is passed on from one generation to the next

group home—a place where people with special needs can live and get their needs met

institution (IN-stuh-TOO-shuhn)—a large home for people who cannot live on their own or with their families

mental illness—an illness of the mind

mental retardation—a condition marked by below average intelligence and development

physical therapy (FIZ-uh-kuhl THER-uh-pee)—treating a disease or disability with exercise or physical activity

seizure (SEE-zhur) **disorders**—brain disorders that result in seizures, or loss of control of muscles

RESOURCES

Autism Research Institute
4182 Adams Avenue
San Diego, CA 92116
(619) 281-7615

Autism Society of America
7910 Woodmont Avenue, Suite 650
Bethesda, MD 20814-3015
(301) 657-0881
www.autism-society.org

CAN (Cure Autism Now)
5225 Wilshire Boulevard, Suite 503
Los Angeles, CA 90036
(213) 549-0500
www.canfoundation.org

Center for the Study of Autism
P. O. Box 4538
Salem, OR 97302
www.autism.org

Learning Disabilities Association
4156 Library Road
Pittsburgh, PA 15234-1349
(412) 341-1515

National Alliance for Autism Research
66 Witherspoon Street, Suite 310
Princeton, NJ 08542
(888) 777-NAAR
www.naar.org

About the **AUTHOR**

Zachary Micah Gartenberg lives in Seattle, Washington, and attends the Jewish Day School of Metropolitan Seattle. He enjoys writing, drawing, sports, and playing with his friends. He worked very hard on this book.

About the **PHOTOGRAPHER**

Jerry Gay's work as a photographer has led him in many directions. He has worked as a photojournalist for various magazines and newspapers. He has also worked in stock photography, publishing, lecturing, and teaching. He has won numerous awards and recognition for his photography. In 1975, while serving as Director of Photography for the Seattle Times, he won the Pulitzer Prize for news photography. The following year he was elected President of the National Press Photographers Association. He lives in Seattle, Washington.